DATE

LOCATION

GPS

WEATHER CONDITIONS

SPECIES / TYPE

SPECIMEN #

TOTAL LENGTH

TYPE OF FOREST

☐ DECIDUOUS	☐ CONIFEROUS
☐ TROPICAL	☐ OTHER

CAP CHARACTERISTICS

CAP COLOR

CAP SHAPE

CAP TEXTURE

CAP DIAMETER

CAP LENGTH

HYMENIUM

SPECIAL PROPERTIES

STALK CHARACTERISTICS

STALK COLOR

STALK SHAPE

STALK TEXTURE

STALK DIAMETER

STALK LENGTH

STALK SURFACE

SPECIAL PROPERTIES

SURROUNDING PLANTS

FAUNA / WILDLIFE

ADDITIONAL NOTES

DATE

LOCATION

GPS

WEATHER CONDITIONS

☐ ☐ ☐ ☐ ☐

SPECIES / TYPE

SPECIMEN #

TOTAL LENGTH

TYPE OF FOREST

☐ DECIDUOUS	☐ CONIFEROUS
☐ TROPICAL	☐ OTHER

CAP CHARACTERISTICS

CAP COLOR

CAP SHAPE

CAP TEXTURE

CAP DIAMETER

CAP LENGTH

HYMENIUM

SPECIAL PROPERTIES

STALK CHARACTERISTICS

STALK COLOR

STALK SHAPE

STALK TEXTURE

STALK DIAMETER

STALK LENGTH

STALK SURFACE

SPECIAL PROPERTIES

SURROUNDING PLANTS

FAUNA / WILDLIFE

ADDITIONAL NOTES

DATE

LOCATION

GPS

WEATHER CONDITIONS

☐ ☐ ☐ ☐ ☐

SPECIES / TYPE

SPECIMEN #

TOTAL LENGTH

TYPE OF FOREST

☐ DECIDUOUS ☐ CONIFEROUS

☐ TROPICAL ☐ OTHER

CAP CHARACTERISTICS

CAP COLOR

CAP SHAPE

CAP TEXTURE

CAP DIAMETER

CAP LENGTH

HYMENIUM

SPECIAL PROPERTIES

STALK CHARACTERISTICS

STALK COLOR

STALK SHAPE

STALK TEXTURE

STALK DIAMETER

STALK LENGTH

STALK SURFACE

SPECIAL PROPERTIES

SURROUNDING PLANTS

FAUNA / WILDLIFE

ADDITIONAL NOTES

DATE

LOCATION

GPS

WEATHER CONDITIONS

SPECIES / TYPE

SPECIMEN #

TOTAL LENGTH

TYPE OF FOREST

- [ ] DECIDUOUS
- [ ] CONIFEROUS
- [ ] TROPICAL
- [ ] OTHER

CAP CHARACTERISTICS

CAP COLOR

CAP SHAPE

CAP TEXTURE

CAP DIAMETER

CAP LENGTH

HYMENIUM

SPECIAL PROPERTIES

STALK CHARACTERISTICS

STALK COLOR

STALK SHAPE

STALK TEXTURE

STALK DIAMETER

STALK LENGTH

STALK SURFACE

SPECIAL PROPERTIES

SURROUNDING PLANTS

FAUNA / WILDLIFE

ADDITIONAL NOTES

DATE	
LOCATION	
GPS	

WEATHER CONDITIONS					
___					
___	☐	☐	☐	☐	☐

SPECIES / TYPE	
SPECIMEN #	
TOTAL LENGTH	

TYPE OF FOREST	
☐ DECIDUOUS	☐ CONIFEROUS
☐ TROPICAL	☐ OTHER

CAP CHARACTERISTICS	
CAP COLOR	
CAP SHAPE	
CAP TEXTURE	
CAP DIAMETER	
CAP LENGTH	
HYMENIUM	
SPECIAL PROPERTIES	

STALK CHARACTERISTICS	
STALK COLOR	
STALK SHAPE	
STALK TEXTURE	
STALK DIAMETER	
STALK LENGTH	
STALK SURFACE	
SPECIAL PROPERTIES	

SURROUNDING PLANTS

FAUNA / WILDLIFE

ADDITIONAL NOTES

DATE

LOCATION

GPS

WEATHER CONDITIONS

SPECIES / TYPE

SPECIMEN #

TOTAL LENGTH

TYPE OF FOREST

☐ DECIDUOUS	☐ CONIFEROUS
☐ TROPICAL	☐ OTHER

CAP CHARACTERISTICS

CAP COLOR

CAP SHAPE

CAP TEXTURE

CAP DIAMETER

CAP LENGTH

HYMENIUM

SPECIAL PROPERTIES

STALK CHARACTERISTICS

STALK COLOR

STALK SHAPE

STALK TEXTURE

STALK DIAMETER

STALK LENGTH

STALK SURFACE

SPECIAL PROPERTIES

SURROUNDING PLANTS

FAUNA / WILDLIFE

ADDITIONAL NOTES

DATE

LOCATION

GPS

WEATHER CONDITIONS

SPECIES / TYPE

SPECIMEN #

TOTAL LENGTH

TYPE OF FOREST

DECIDUOUS	CONIFEROUS
TROPICAL	OTHER

CAP CHARACTERISTICS

CAP COLOR

CAP SHAPE

CAP TEXTURE

CAP DIAMETER

CAP LENGTH

HYMENIUM

SPECIAL PROPERTIES

STALK CHARACTERISTICS

STALK COLOR

STALK SHAPE

STALK TEXTURE

STALK DIAMETER

STALK LENGTH

STALK SURFACE

SPECIAL PROPERTIES

SURROUNDING PLANTS

FAUNA / WILDLIFE

ADDITIONAL NOTES

DATE
LOCATION
GPS

WEATHER CONDITIONS
___
___

SPECIES / TYPE
SPECIMEN #
TOTAL LENGTH

TYPE OF FOREST	
☐ DECIDUOUS	☐ CONIFEROUS
☐ TROPICAL	☐ OTHER

CAP CHARACTERISTICS
CAP COLOR
CAP SHAPE
CAP TEXTURE
CAP DIAMETER
CAP LENGTH
HYMENIUM
SPECIAL PROPERTIES

STALK CHARACTERISTICS
STALK COLOR
STALK SHAPE
STALK TEXTURE
STALK DIAMETER
STALK LENGTH
STALK SURFACE
SPECIAL PROPERTIES

SURROUNDING PLANTS

FAUNA / WILDLIFE

ADDITIONAL NOTES

DATE
LOCATION
GPS

WEATHER CONDITIONS
___
___ ☐ ☐ ☐ ☐ ☐

SPECIES / TYPE
SPECIMEN #
TOTAL LENGTH

TYPE OF FOREST	
☐ DECIDUOUS	☐ CONIFEROUS
☐ TROPICAL	☐ OTHER

CAP CHARACTERISTICS
CAP COLOR
CAP SHAPE
CAP TEXTURE
CAP DIAMETER
CAP LENGTH
HYMENIUM
SPECIAL PROPERTIES

STALK CHARACTERISTICS
STALK COLOR
STALK SHAPE
STALK TEXTURE
STALK DIAMETER
STALK LENGTH
STALK SURFACE
SPECIAL PROPERTIES

SURROUNDING PLANTS

FAUNA / WILDLIFE

ADDITIONAL NOTES

DATE

LOCATION

GPS

WEATHER CONDITIONS

SPECIES / TYPE

SPECIMEN #

TOTAL LENGTH

TYPE OF FOREST

☐ DECIDUOUS	☐ CONIFEROUS
☐ TROPICAL	☐ OTHER

CAP CHARACTERISTICS

CAP COLOR

CAP SHAPE

CAP TEXTURE

CAP DIAMETER

CAP LENGTH

HYMENIUM

SPECIAL PROPERTIES

STALK CHARACTERISTICS

STALK COLOR

STALK SHAPE

STALK TEXTURE

STALK DIAMETER

STALK LENGTH

STALK SURFACE

SPECIAL PROPERTIES

SURROUNDING PLANTS

FAUNA / WILDLIFE

ADDITIONAL NOTES

DATE

LOCATION

GPS

WEATHER CONDITIONS

SPECIES / TYPE

SPECIMEN #

TOTAL LENGTH

TYPE OF FOREST

- [ ] DECIDUOUS
- [ ] CONIFEROUS
- [ ] TROPICAL
- [ ] OTHER

CAP CHARACTERISTICS

CAP COLOR

CAP SHAPE

CAP TEXTURE

CAP DIAMETER

CAP LENGTH

HYMENIUM

SPECIAL PROPERTIES

STALK CHARACTERISTICS

STALK COLOR

STALK SHAPE

STALK TEXTURE

STALK DIAMETER

STALK LENGTH

STALK SURFACE

SPECIAL PROPERTIES

SURROUNDING PLANTS

FAUNA / WILDLIFE

ADDITIONAL NOTES

DATE
LOCATION
GPS

WEATHER CONDITIONS						
Temperature	____	☐ Sunny	☐ Partly cloudy	☐ Rain	☐ Storm	☐ Snow
Wind	____					

SPECIES / TYPE
SPECIMEN #
TOTAL LENGTH

TYPE OF FOREST	
☐ DECIDUOUS	☐ CONIFEROUS
☐ TROPICAL	☐ OTHER

CAP CHARACTERISTICS
CAP COLOR
CAP SHAPE
CAP TEXTURE
CAP DIAMETER
CAP LENGTH
HYMENIUM
SPECIAL PROPERTIES

STALK CHARACTERISTICS
STALK COLOR
STALK SHAPE
STALK TEXTURE
STALK DIAMETER
STALK LENGTH
STALK SURFACE
SPECIAL PROPERTIES

SURROUNDING PLANTS

FAUNA / WILDLIFE

ADDITIONAL NOTES

DATE
LOCATION
GPS

WEATHER CONDITIONS
___
___ ☐ ☐ ☐ ☐ ☐

SPECIES / TYPE
SPECIMEN #
TOTAL LENGTH

TYPE OF FOREST	
☐ DECIDUOUS	☐ CONIFEROUS
☐ TROPICAL	☐ OTHER

CAP CHARACTERISTICS
CAP COLOR
CAP SHAPE
CAP TEXTURE
CAP DIAMETER
CAP LENGTH
HYMENIUM
SPECIAL PROPERTIES

STALK CHARACTERISTICS
STALK COLOR
STALK SHAPE
STALK TEXTURE
STALK DIAMETER
STALK LENGTH
STALK SURFACE
SPECIAL PROPERTIES

SURROUNDING PLANTS

FAUNA / WILDLIFE

ADDITIONAL NOTES

DATE

LOCATION

GPS

WEATHER CONDITIONS

SPECIES / TYPE

SPECIMEN #

TOTAL LENGTH

TYPE OF FOREST

- DECIDUOUS
- CONIFEROUS
- TROPICAL
- OTHER

CAP CHARACTERISTICS

CAP COLOR

CAP SHAPE

CAP TEXTURE

CAP DIAMETER

CAP LENGTH

HYMENIUM

SPECIAL PROPERTIES

STALK CHARACTERISTICS

STALK COLOR

STALK SHAPE

STALK TEXTURE

STALK DIAMETER

STALK LENGTH

STALK SURFACE

SPECIAL PROPERTIES

SURROUNDING PLANTS

FAUNA / WILDLIFE

ADDITIONAL NOTES

DATE

LOCATION

GPS

WEATHER CONDITIONS

SPECIES / TYPE

SPECIMEN #

TOTAL LENGTH

TYPE OF FOREST

☐ DECIDUOUS	☐ CONIFEROUS
☐ TROPICAL	☐ OTHER

CAP CHARACTERISTICS

CAP COLOR

CAP SHAPE

CAP TEXTURE

CAP DIAMETER

CAP LENGTH

HYMENIUM

SPECIAL PROPERTIES

STALK CHARACTERISTICS

STALK COLOR

STALK SHAPE

STALK TEXTURE

STALK DIAMETER

STALK LENGTH

STALK SURFACE

SPECIAL PROPERTIES

SURROUNDING PLANTS

FAUNA / WILDLIFE

ADDITIONAL NOTES

DATE

LOCATION

GPS

WEATHER CONDITIONS

SPECIES / TYPE

SPECIMEN #

TOTAL LENGTH

TYPE OF FOREST

☐ DECIDUOUS	☐ CONIFEROUS
☐ TROPICAL	☐ OTHER

CAP CHARACTERISTICS

CAP COLOR

CAP SHAPE

CAP TEXTURE

CAP DIAMETER

CAP LENGTH

HYMENIUM

SPECIAL PROPERTIES

STALK CHARACTERISTICS

STALK COLOR

STALK SHAPE

STALK TEXTURE

STALK DIAMETER

STALK LENGTH

STALK SURFACE

SPECIAL PROPERTIES

SURROUNDING PLANTS

FAUNA / WILDLIFE

ADDITIONAL NOTES

DATE	
LOCATION	
GPS	

WEATHER CONDITIONS

SPECIES / TYPE

SPECIES / TYPE	
SPECIMEN #	
TOTAL LENGTH	

TYPE OF FOREST

☐ DECIDUOUS	☐ CONIFEROUS
☐ TROPICAL	☐ OTHER

CAP CHARACTERISTICS

- CAP COLOR
- CAP SHAPE
- CAP TEXTURE
- CAP DIAMETER
- CAP LENGTH
- HYMENIUM
- SPECIAL PROPERTIES

STALK CHARACTERISTICS

- STALK COLOR
- STALK SHAPE
- STALK TEXTURE
- STALK DIAMETER
- STALK LENGTH
- STALK SURFACE
- SPECIAL PROPERTIES

SURROUNDING PLANTS

FAUNA / WILDLIFE

ADDITIONAL NOTES

DATE
LOCATION
GPS

WEATHER CONDITIONS
___ ☐ ☐ ☐ ☐ ☐

SPECIES / TYPE
SPECIMEN #
TOTAL LENGTH

TYPE OF FOREST	
☐ DECIDUOUS	☐ CONIFEROUS
☐ TROPICAL	☐ OTHER

CAP CHARACTERISTICS
CAP COLOR
CAP SHAPE
CAP TEXTURE
CAP DIAMETER
CAP LENGTH
HYMENIUM
SPECIAL PROPERTIES

STALK CHARACTERISTICS
STALK COLOR
STALK SHAPE
STALK TEXTURE
STALK DIAMETER
STALK LENGTH
STALK SURFACE
SPECIAL PROPERTIES

SURROUNDING PLANTS

FAUNA / WILDLIFE

ADDITIONAL NOTES

DATE
LOCATION
GPS

WEATHER CONDITIONS						
	___	☐	☐	☐	☐	☐

SPECIES / TYPE
SPECIMEN #
TOTAL LENGTH

TYPE OF FOREST	
☐ DECIDUOUS	☐ CONIFEROUS
☐ TROPICAL	☐ OTHER

CAP CHARACTERISTICS
CAP COLOR
CAP SHAPE
CAP TEXTURE
CAP DIAMETER
CAP LENGTH
HYMENIUM
SPECIAL PROPERTIES

STALK CHARACTERISTICS
STALK COLOR
STALK SHAPE
STALK TEXTURE
STALK DIAMETER
STALK LENGTH
STALK SURFACE
SPECIAL PROPERTIES

SURROUNDING PLANTS

FAUNA / WILDLIFE

ADDITIONAL NOTES

DATE
LOCATION
GPS

WEATHER CONDITIONS

SPECIES / TYPE
SPECIMEN #
TOTAL LENGTH

TYPE OF FOREST	
☐ DECIDUOUS	☐ CONIFEROUS
☐ TROPICAL	☐ OTHER

CAP CHARACTERISTICS
CAP COLOR
CAP SHAPE
CAP TEXTURE
CAP DIAMETER
CAP LENGTH
HYMENIUM
SPECIAL PROPERTIES

STALK CHARACTERISTICS
STALK COLOR
STALK SHAPE
STALK TEXTURE
STALK DIAMETER
STALK LENGTH
STALK SURFACE
SPECIAL PROPERTIES

SURROUNDING PLANTS

FAUNA / WILDLIFE

ADDITIONAL NOTES

DATE
LOCATION
GPS

WEATHER CONDITIONS

SPECIES / TYPE
SPECIMEN #
TOTAL LENGTH

TYPE OF FOREST	
DECIDUOUS	CONIFEROUS
TROPICAL	OTHER

CAP CHARACTERISTICS
CAP COLOR
CAP SHAPE
CAP TEXTURE
CAP DIAMETER
CAP LENGTH
HYMENIUM
SPECIAL PROPERTIES

STALK CHARACTERISTICS
STALK COLOR
STALK SHAPE
STALK TEXTURE
STALK DIAMETER
STALK LENGTH
STALK SURFACE
SPECIAL PROPERTIES

SURROUNDING PLANTS

FAUNA / WILDLIFE

ADDITIONAL NOTES

DATE
LOCATION
GPS

WEATHER CONDITIONS
___ ☐ ☐ ☐ ☐ ☐

SPECIES / TYPE
SPECIMEN #
TOTAL LENGTH

TYPE OF FOREST	
☐ DECIDUOUS	☐ CONIFEROUS
☐ TROPICAL	☐ OTHER

CAP CHARACTERISTICS
CAP COLOR
CAP SHAPE
CAP TEXTURE
CAP DIAMETER
CAP LENGTH
HYMENIUM
SPECIAL PROPERTIES

STALK CHARACTERISTICS
STALK COLOR
STALK SHAPE
STALK TEXTURE
STALK DIAMETER
STALK LENGTH
STALK SURFACE
SPECIAL PROPERTIES

SURROUNDING PLANTS

FAUNA / WILDLIFE

ADDITIONAL NOTES

DATE	WEATHER CONDITIONS
LOCATION	
GPS	

SPECIES / TYPE
SPECIMEN #
TOTAL LENGTH

TYPE OF FOREST	
☐ DECIDUOUS	☐ CONIFEROUS
☐ TROPICAL	☐ OTHER

CAP CHARACTERISTICS
CAP COLOR
CAP SHAPE
CAP TEXTURE
CAP DIAMETER
CAP LENGTH
HYMENIUM
SPECIAL PROPERTIES

STALK CHARACTERISTICS
STALK COLOR
STALK SHAPE
STALK TEXTURE
STALK DIAMETER
STALK LENGTH
STALK SURFACE
SPECIAL PROPERTIES

SURROUNDING PLANTS

FAUNA / WILDLIFE

ADDITIONAL NOTES

DATE
LOCATION
GPS

WEATHER CONDITIONS
___ ☐ ☐ ☐ ☐ ☐
___ ☐ ☐ ☐ ☐ ☐

SPECIES / TYPE
SPECIMEN #
TOTAL LENGTH

TYPE OF FOREST	
☐ DECIDUOUS	☐ CONIFEROUS
☐ TROPICAL	☐ OTHER

CAP CHARACTERISTICS
CAP COLOR
CAP SHAPE
CAP TEXTURE
CAP DIAMETER
CAP LENGTH
HYMENIUM
SPECIAL PROPERTIES

STALK CHARACTERISTICS
STALK COLOR
STALK SHAPE
STALK TEXTURE
STALK DIAMETER
STALK LENGTH
STALK SURFACE
SPECIAL PROPERTIES

SURROUNDING PLANTS

FAUNA / WILDLIFE

ADDITIONAL NOTES

DATE
LOCATION
GPS

WEATHER CONDITIONS

SPECIES / TYPE
SPECIMEN #
TOTAL LENGTH

TYPE OF FOREST	
☐ DECIDUOUS	☐ CONIFEROUS
☐ TROPICAL	☐ OTHER

CAP CHARACTERISTICS
CAP COLOR
CAP SHAPE
CAP TEXTURE
CAP DIAMETER
CAP LENGTH
HYMENIUM
SPECIAL PROPERTIES

STALK CHARACTERISTICS
STALK COLOR
STALK SHAPE
STALK TEXTURE
STALK DIAMETER
STALK LENGTH
STALK SURFACE
SPECIAL PROPERTIES

SURROUNDING PLANTS

FAUNA / WILDLIFE

ADDITIONAL NOTES

DATE
LOCATION
GPS

WEATHER CONDITIONS
___ ☐ ☐ ☐ ☐ ☐
___

SPECIES / TYPE
SPECIMEN #
TOTAL LENGTH

TYPE OF FOREST	
☐ DECIDUOUS	☐ CONIFEROUS
☐ TROPICAL	☐ OTHER

CAP CHARACTERISTICS
CAP COLOR
CAP SHAPE
CAP TEXTURE
CAP DIAMETER
CAP LENGTH
HYMENIUM
SPECIAL PROPERTIES

STALK CHARACTERISTICS
STALK COLOR
STALK SHAPE
STALK TEXTURE
STALK DIAMETER
STALK LENGTH
STALK SURFACE
SPECIAL PROPERTIES

SURROUNDING PLANTS

FAUNA / WILDLIFE

ADDITIONAL NOTES

DATE
LOCATION
GPS

WEATHER CONDITIONS

SPECIES / TYPE
SPECIMEN #
TOTAL LENGTH

TYPE OF FOREST	
☐ DECIDUOUS	☐ CONIFEROUS
☐ TROPICAL	☐ OTHER

CAP CHARACTERISTICS
CAP COLOR
CAP SHAPE
CAP TEXTURE
CAP DIAMETER
CAP LENGTH
HYMENIUM
SPECIAL PROPERTIES

STALK CHARACTERISTICS
STALK COLOR
STALK SHAPE
STALK TEXTURE
STALK DIAMETER
STALK LENGTH
STALK SURFACE
SPECIAL PROPERTIES

SURROUNDING PLANTS

FAUNA / WILDLIFE

ADDITIONAL NOTES

DATE

LOCATION

GPS

WEATHER CONDITIONS

SPECIES / TYPE

SPECIMEN #

TOTAL LENGTH

TYPE OF FOREST

- [ ] DECIDUOUS
- [ ] CONIFEROUS
- [ ] TROPICAL
- [ ] OTHER

CAP CHARACTERISTICS

CAP COLOR

CAP SHAPE

CAP TEXTURE

CAP DIAMETER

CAP LENGTH

HYMENIUM

SPECIAL PROPERTIES

STALK CHARACTERISTICS

STALK COLOR

STALK SHAPE

STALK TEXTURE

STALK DIAMETER

STALK LENGTH

STALK SURFACE

SPECIAL PROPERTIES

SURROUNDING PLANTS

FAUNA / WILDLIFE

ADDITIONAL NOTES

DATE

LOCATION

GPS

WEATHER CONDITIONS

SPECIES / TYPE

SPECIMEN #

TOTAL LENGTH

TYPE OF FOREST

☐ DECIDUOUS	☐ CONIFEROUS
☐ TROPICAL	☐ OTHER

CAP CHARACTERISTICS

CAP COLOR

CAP SHAPE

CAP TEXTURE

CAP DIAMETER

CAP LENGTH

HYMENIUM

SPECIAL PROPERTIES

STALK CHARACTERISTICS

STALK COLOR

STALK SHAPE

STALK TEXTURE

STALK DIAMETER

STALK LENGTH

STALK SURFACE

SPECIAL PROPERTIES

SURROUNDING PLANTS

FAUNA / WILDLIFE

ADDITIONAL NOTES

DATE
LOCATION
GPS

WEATHER CONDITIONS
___ ☐ ☐ ☐ ☐ ☐
___

SPECIES / TYPE
SPECIMEN #
TOTAL LENGTH

TYPE OF FOREST	
☐ DECIDUOUS	☐ CONIFEROUS
☐ TROPICAL	☐ OTHER

CAP CHARACTERISTICS
CAP COLOR
CAP SHAPE
CAP TEXTURE
CAP DIAMETER
CAP LENGTH
HYMENIUM
SPECIAL PROPERTIES

STALK CHARACTERISTICS
STALK COLOR
STALK SHAPE
STALK TEXTURE
STALK DIAMETER
STALK LENGTH
STALK SURFACE
SPECIAL PROPERTIES

SURROUNDING PLANTS

FAUNA / WILDLIFE

ADDITIONAL NOTES

DATE	
LOCATION	
GPS	

WEATHER CONDITIONS
___
___ ☐ ☐ ☐ ☐ ☐

SPECIES / TYPE	
SPECIMEN #	
TOTAL LENGTH	

TYPE OF FOREST	
☐ DECIDUOUS	☐ CONIFEROUS
☐ TROPICAL	☐ OTHER

CAP CHARACTERISTICS	
CAP COLOR	
CAP SHAPE	
CAP TEXTURE	
CAP DIAMETER	
CAP LENGTH	
HYMENIUM	
SPECIAL PROPERTIES	

STALK CHARACTERISTICS	
STALK COLOR	
STALK SHAPE	
STALK TEXTURE	
STALK DIAMETER	
STALK LENGTH	
STALK SURFACE	
SPECIAL PROPERTIES	

SURROUNDING PLANTS

FAUNA / WILDLIFE

ADDITIONAL NOTES

DATE
LOCATION
GPS

WEATHER CONDITIONS

SPECIES / TYPE
SPECIMEN #
TOTAL LENGTH

TYPE OF FOREST	
☐ DECIDUOUS	☐ CONIFEROUS
☐ TROPICAL	☐ OTHER

CAP CHARACTERISTICS
CAP COLOR
CAP SHAPE
CAP TEXTURE
CAP DIAMETER
CAP LENGTH
HYMENIUM
SPECIAL PROPERTIES

STALK CHARACTERISTICS
STALK COLOR
STALK SHAPE
STALK TEXTURE
STALK DIAMETER
STALK LENGTH
STALK SURFACE
SPECIAL PROPERTIES

SURROUNDING PLANTS

FAUNA / WILDLIFE

ADDITIONAL NOTES

DATE
LOCATION
GPS

WEATHER CONDITIONS
___
___

SPECIES / TYPE
SPECIMEN #
TOTAL LENGTH

TYPE OF FOREST	
DECIDUOUS	CONIFEROUS
TROPICAL	OTHER

CAP CHARACTERISTICS
CAP COLOR
CAP SHAPE
CAP TEXTURE
CAP DIAMETER
CAP LENGTH
HYMENIUM
SPECIAL PROPERTIES

STALK CHARACTERISTICS
STALK COLOR
STALK SHAPE
STALK TEXTURE
STALK DIAMETER
STALK LENGTH
STALK SURFACE
SPECIAL PROPERTIES

SURROUNDING PLANTS

FAUNA / WILDLIFE

ADDITIONAL NOTES

DATE

LOCATION

GPS

WEATHER CONDITIONS

SPECIES / TYPE

SPECIMEN #

TOTAL LENGTH

TYPE OF FOREST

☐ DECIDUOUS	☐ CONIFEROUS
☐ TROPICAL	☐ OTHER

CAP CHARACTERISTICS

CAP COLOR

CAP SHAPE

CAP TEXTURE

CAP DIAMETER

CAP LENGTH

HYMENIUM

SPECIAL PROPERTIES

STALK CHARACTERISTICS

STALK COLOR

STALK SHAPE

STALK TEXTURE

STALK DIAMETER

STALK LENGTH

STALK SURFACE

SPECIAL PROPERTIES

SURROUNDING PLANTS

FAUNA / WILDLIFE

ADDITIONAL NOTES

DATE
LOCATION
GPS

WEATHER CONDITIONS
Temperature: ____ ☐ sunny ☐ partly cloudy ☐ rain ☐ storm ☐ snow
Wind: ____

SPECIES / TYPE
SPECIMEN #
TOTAL LENGTH

TYPE OF FOREST	
☐ DECIDUOUS	☐ CONIFEROUS
☐ TROPICAL	☐ OTHER

CAP CHARACTERISTICS
CAP COLOR
CAP SHAPE
CAP TEXTURE
CAP DIAMETER
CAP LENGTH
HYMENIUM
SPECIAL PROPERTIES

STALK CHARACTERISTICS
STALK COLOR
STALK SHAPE
STALK TEXTURE
STALK DIAMETER
STALK LENGTH
STALK SURFACE
SPECIAL PROPERTIES

SURROUNDING PLANTS

FAUNA / WILDLIFE

ADDITIONAL NOTES

DATE

LOCATION

GPS

WEATHER CONDITIONS

SPECIES / TYPE

SPECIMEN #

TOTAL LENGTH

TYPE OF FOREST

☐ DECIDUOUS	☐ CONIFEROUS
☐ TROPICAL	☐ OTHER

CAP CHARACTERISTICS

CAP COLOR

CAP SHAPE

CAP TEXTURE

CAP DIAMETER

CAP LENGTH

HYMENIUM

SPECIAL PROPERTIES

STALK CHARACTERISTICS

STALK COLOR

STALK SHAPE

STALK TEXTURE

STALK DIAMETER

STALK LENGTH

STALK SURFACE

SPECIAL PROPERTIES

SURROUNDING PLANTS

FAUNA / WILDLIFE

ADDITIONAL NOTES

DATE
LOCATION
GPS

WEATHER CONDITIONS

SPECIES / TYPE
SPECIMEN #
TOTAL LENGTH

TYPE OF FOREST	
☐ DECIDUOUS	☐ CONIFEROUS
☐ TROPICAL	☐ OTHER

CAP CHARACTERISTICS
CAP COLOR
CAP SHAPE
CAP TEXTURE
CAP DIAMETER
CAP LENGTH
HYMENIUM
SPECIAL PROPERTIES

STALK CHARACTERISTICS
STALK COLOR
STALK SHAPE
STALK TEXTURE
STALK DIAMETER
STALK LENGTH
STALK SURFACE
SPECIAL PROPERTIES

SURROUNDING PLANTS

FAUNA / WILDLIFE

ADDITIONAL NOTES

DATE

LOCATION

GPS

WEATHER CONDITIONS

SPECIES / TYPE

SPECIMEN #

TOTAL LENGTH

TYPE OF FOREST

- ☐ DECIDUOUS
- ☐ CONIFEROUS
- ☐ TROPICAL
- ☐ OTHER

CAP CHARACTERISTICS

CAP COLOR

CAP SHAPE

CAP TEXTURE

CAP DIAMETER

CAP LENGTH

HYMENIUM

SPECIAL PROPERTIES

STALK CHARACTERISTICS

STALK COLOR

STALK SHAPE

STALK TEXTURE

STALK DIAMETER

STALK LENGTH

STALK SURFACE

SPECIAL PROPERTIES

SURROUNDING PLANTS

FAUNA / WILDLIFE

ADDITIONAL NOTES

DATE
LOCATION
GPS

WEATHER CONDITIONS

SPECIES / TYPE
SPECIMEN #
TOTAL LENGTH

TYPE OF FOREST	
☐ DECIDUOUS	☐ CONIFEROUS
☐ TROPICAL	☐ OTHER

CAP CHARACTERISTICS
CAP COLOR
CAP SHAPE
CAP TEXTURE
CAP DIAMETER
CAP LENGTH
HYMENIUM
SPECIAL PROPERTIES

STALK CHARACTERISTICS
STALK COLOR
STALK SHAPE
STALK TEXTURE
STALK DIAMETER
STALK LENGTH
STALK SURFACE
SPECIAL PROPERTIES

SURROUNDING PLANTS

FAUNA / WILDLIFE

ADDITIONAL NOTES

DATE

LOCATION

GPS

WEATHER CONDITIONS

SPECIES / TYPE

SPECIMEN #

TOTAL LENGTH

TYPE OF FOREST

☐ DECIDUOUS	☐ CONIFEROUS
☐ TROPICAL	☐ OTHER

CAP CHARACTERISTICS

CAP COLOR

CAP SHAPE

CAP TEXTURE

CAP DIAMETER

CAP LENGTH

HYMENIUM

SPECIAL PROPERTIES

STALK CHARACTERISTICS

STALK COLOR

STALK SHAPE

STALK TEXTURE

STALK DIAMETER

STALK LENGTH

STALK SURFACE

SPECIAL PROPERTIES

SURROUNDING PLANTS

FAUNA / WILDLIFE

ADDITIONAL NOTES

DATE
LOCATION
GPS

WEATHER CONDITIONS
___
___

SPECIES / TYPE
SPECIMEN #
TOTAL LENGTH

TYPE OF FOREST	
☐ DECIDUOUS	☐ CONIFEROUS
☐ TROPICAL	☐ OTHER

CAP CHARACTERISTICS
CAP COLOR
CAP SHAPE
CAP TEXTURE
CAP DIAMETER
CAP LENGTH
HYMENIUM
SPECIAL PROPERTIES

STALK CHARACTERISTICS
STALK COLOR
STALK SHAPE
STALK TEXTURE
STALK DIAMETER
STALK LENGTH
STALK SURFACE
SPECIAL PROPERTIES

SURROUNDING PLANTS

FAUNA / WILDLIFE

ADDITIONAL NOTES

DATE

LOCATION

GPS

WEATHER CONDITIONS

____	☐	☐	☐	☐	☐

SPECIES / TYPE

SPECIMEN #

TOTAL LENGTH

TYPE OF FOREST

☐ DECIDUOUS	☐ CONIFEROUS
☐ TROPICAL	☐ OTHER

CAP CHARACTERISTICS

CAP COLOR

CAP SHAPE

CAP TEXTURE

CAP DIAMETER

CAP LENGTH

HYMENIUM

SPECIAL PROPERTIES

STALK CHARACTERISTICS

STALK COLOR

STALK SHAPE

STALK TEXTURE

STALK DIAMETER

STALK LENGTH

STALK SURFACE

SPECIAL PROPERTIES

SURROUNDING PLANTS

FAUNA / WILDLIFE

ADDITIONAL NOTES

DATE

LOCATION

GPS

WEATHER CONDITIONS

SPECIES / TYPE

SPECIMEN #

TOTAL LENGTH

TYPE OF FOREST

- [ ] DECIDUOUS
- [ ] CONIFEROUS
- [ ] TROPICAL
- [ ] OTHER

CAP CHARACTERISTICS

CAP COLOR

CAP SHAPE

CAP TEXTURE

CAP DIAMETER

CAP LENGTH

HYMENIUM

SPECIAL PROPERTIES

STALK CHARACTERISTICS

STALK COLOR

STALK SHAPE

STALK TEXTURE

STALK DIAMETER

STALK LENGTH

STALK SURFACE

SPECIAL PROPERTIES

SURROUNDING PLANTS

FAUNA / WILDLIFE

ADDITIONAL NOTES

DATE
LOCATION
GPS

WEATHER CONDITIONS
____ ☐ ☐ ☐ ☐ ☐
____

SPECIES / TYPE
SPECIMEN #
TOTAL LENGTH

TYPE OF FOREST	
☐ DECIDUOUS	☐ CONIFEROUS
☐ TROPICAL	☐ OTHER

CAP CHARACTERISTICS
CAP COLOR
CAP SHAPE
CAP TEXTURE
CAP DIAMETER
CAP LENGTH
HYMENIUM
SPECIAL PROPERTIES

STALK CHARACTERISTICS
STALK COLOR
STALK SHAPE
STALK TEXTURE
STALK DIAMETER
STALK LENGTH
STALK SURFACE
SPECIAL PROPERTIES

SURROUNDING PLANTS

FAUNA / WILDLIFE

ADDITIONAL NOTES

DATE	
LOCATION	
GPS	

WEATHER CONDITIONS					
____	☐	☐	☐	☐	☐
____					

SPECIES / TYPE	
SPECIMEN #	
TOTAL LENGTH	

TYPE OF FOREST	
☐ DECIDUOUS	☐ CONIFEROUS
☐ TROPICAL	☐ OTHER

CAP CHARACTERISTICS	
CAP COLOR	
CAP SHAPE	
CAP TEXTURE	
CAP DIAMETER	
CAP LENGTH	
HYMENIUM	
SPECIAL PROPERTIES	

STALK CHARACTERISTICS	
STALK COLOR	
STALK SHAPE	
STALK TEXTURE	
STALK DIAMETER	
STALK LENGTH	
STALK SURFACE	
SPECIAL PROPERTIES	

SURROUNDING PLANTS

FAUNA / WILDLIFE

ADDITIONAL NOTES

DATE

LOCATION

GPS

WEATHER CONDITIONS

☐ ☐ ☐ ☐ ☐

SPECIES / TYPE

SPECIMEN #

TOTAL LENGTH

TYPE OF FOREST

☐ DECIDUOUS	☐ CONIFEROUS
☐ TROPICAL	☐ OTHER

CAP CHARACTERISTICS

CAP COLOR

CAP SHAPE

CAP TEXTURE

CAP DIAMETER

CAP LENGTH

HYMENIUM

SPECIAL PROPERTIES

STALK CHARACTERISTICS

STALK COLOR

STALK SHAPE

STALK TEXTURE

STALK DIAMETER

STALK LENGTH

STALK SURFACE

SPECIAL PROPERTIES

SURROUNDING PLANTS

FAUNA / WILDLIFE

ADDITIONAL NOTES

DATE
LOCATION
GPS

WEATHER CONDITIONS

SPECIES / TYPE
SPECIMEN #
TOTAL LENGTH

TYPE OF FOREST	
☐ DECIDUOUS	☐ CONIFEROUS
☐ TROPICAL	☐ OTHER

CAP CHARACTERISTICS
CAP COLOR
CAP SHAPE
CAP TEXTURE
CAP DIAMETER
CAP LENGTH
HYMENIUM
SPECIAL PROPERTIES

STALK CHARACTERISTICS
STALK COLOR
STALK SHAPE
STALK TEXTURE
STALK DIAMETER
STALK LENGTH
STALK SURFACE
SPECIAL PROPERTIES

SURROUNDING PLANTS

FAUNA / WILDLIFE

ADDITIONAL NOTES

DATE
LOCATION
GPS

WEATHER CONDITIONS					
____	☐	☐	☐	☐	☐
____					

SPECIES / TYPE
SPECIMEN #
TOTAL LENGTH

TYPE OF FOREST	
☐ DECIDUOUS	☐ CONIFEROUS
☐ TROPICAL	☐ OTHER

CAP CHARACTERISTICS
CAP COLOR
CAP SHAPE
CAP TEXTURE
CAP DIAMETER
CAP LENGTH
HYMENIUM
SPECIAL PROPERTIES

STALK CHARACTERISTICS
STALK COLOR
STALK SHAPE
STALK TEXTURE
STALK DIAMETER
STALK LENGTH
STALK SURFACE
SPECIAL PROPERTIES

SURROUNDING PLANTS

FAUNA / WILDLIFE

ADDITIONAL NOTES

DATE
LOCATION
GPS

WEATHER CONDITIONS

SPECIES / TYPE
SPECIMEN #
TOTAL LENGTH

TYPE OF FOREST	
☐ DECIDUOUS	☐ CONIFEROUS
☐ TROPICAL	☐ OTHER

CAP CHARACTERISTICS
CAP COLOR
CAP SHAPE
CAP TEXTURE
CAP DIAMETER
CAP LENGTH
HYMENIUM
SPECIAL PROPERTIES

STALK CHARACTERISTICS
STALK COLOR
STALK SHAPE
STALK TEXTURE
STALK DIAMETER
STALK LENGTH
STALK SURFACE
SPECIAL PROPERTIES

SURROUNDING PLANTS

FAUNA / WILDLIFE

ADDITIONAL NOTES

DATE
LOCATION
GPS

WEATHER CONDITIONS
☐ ☐ ☐ ☐ ☐

SPECIES / TYPE
SPECIMEN #
TOTAL LENGTH

TYPE OF FOREST	
☐ DECIDUOUS	☐ CONIFEROUS
☐ TROPICAL	☐ OTHER

CAP CHARACTERISTICS
CAP COLOR
CAP SHAPE
CAP TEXTURE
CAP DIAMETER
CAP LENGTH
HYMENIUM
SPECIAL PROPERTIES

STALK CHARACTERISTICS
STALK COLOR
STALK SHAPE
STALK TEXTURE
STALK DIAMETER
STALK LENGTH
STALK SURFACE
SPECIAL PROPERTIES

SURROUNDING PLANTS

FAUNA / WILDLIFE

ADDITIONAL NOTES

DATE	
LOCATION	
GPS	

WEATHER CONDITIONS

___	☐	☐	☐	☐	☐
___					

SPECIES / TYPE	
SPECIMEN #	
TOTAL LENGTH	

TYPE OF FOREST

☐ DECIDUOUS	☐ CONIFEROUS
☐ TROPICAL	☐ OTHER

CAP CHARACTERISTICS

CAP COLOR	
CAP SHAPE	
CAP TEXTURE	
CAP DIAMETER	
CAP LENGTH	
HYMENIUM	
SPECIAL PROPERTIES	

STALK CHARACTERISTICS

STALK COLOR	
STALK SHAPE	
STALK TEXTURE	
STALK DIAMETER	
STALK LENGTH	
STALK SURFACE	
SPECIAL PROPERTIES	

SURROUNDING PLANTS

FAUNA / WILDLIFE

ADDITIONAL NOTES

DATE
LOCATION
GPS

WEATHER CONDITIONS

SPECIES / TYPE
SPECIMEN #
TOTAL LENGTH

TYPE OF FOREST	
☐ DECIDUOUS	☐ CONIFEROUS
☐ TROPICAL	☐ OTHER

CAP CHARACTERISTICS
CAP COLOR
CAP SHAPE
CAP TEXTURE
CAP DIAMETER
CAP LENGTH
HYMENIUM
SPECIAL PROPERTIES

STALK CHARACTERISTICS
STALK COLOR
STALK SHAPE
STALK TEXTURE
STALK DIAMETER
STALK LENGTH
STALK SURFACE
SPECIAL PROPERTIES

SURROUNDING PLANTS

FAUNA / WILDLIFE

ADDITIONAL NOTES

DATE	
LOCATION	
GPS	

WEATHER CONDITIONS					
____					
____	☐	☐	☐	☐	☐

SPECIES / TYPE	
SPECIMEN #	
TOTAL LENGTH	

TYPE OF FOREST	
☐ DECIDUOUS	☐ CONIFEROUS
☐ TROPICAL	☐ OTHER

CAP CHARACTERISTICS	
CAP COLOR	
CAP SHAPE	
CAP TEXTURE	
CAP DIAMETER	
CAP LENGTH	
HYMENIUM	
SPECIAL PROPERTIES	

STALK CHARACTERISTICS	
STALK COLOR	
STALK SHAPE	
STALK TEXTURE	
STALK DIAMETER	
STALK LENGTH	
STALK SURFACE	
SPECIAL PROPERTIES	

SURROUNDING PLANTS

FAUNA / WILDLIFE

ADDITIONAL NOTES

DATE	
LOCATION	
GPS	

WEATHER CONDITIONS
☐ ☐ ☐ ☐ ☐

SPECIES / TYPE	
SPECIMEN #	
TOTAL LENGTH	

TYPE OF FOREST	
☐ DECIDUOUS	☐ CONIFEROUS
☐ TROPICAL	☐ OTHER

CAP CHARACTERISTICS	
CAP COLOR	
CAP SHAPE	
CAP TEXTURE	
CAP DIAMETER	
CAP LENGTH	
HYMENIUM	
SPECIAL PROPERTIES	

STALK CHARACTERISTICS	
STALK COLOR	
STALK SHAPE	
STALK TEXTURE	
STALK DIAMETER	
STALK LENGTH	
STALK SURFACE	
SPECIAL PROPERTIES	

SURROUNDING PLANTS

FAUNA / WILDLIFE

ADDITIONAL NOTES

DATE
LOCATION
GPS

WEATHER CONDITIONS
___ ☐ ☐ ☐ ☐ ☐
___ ☐ ☐ ☐ ☐ ☐

SPECIES / TYPE
SPECIMEN #
TOTAL LENGTH

TYPE OF FOREST	
☐ DECIDUOUS	☐ CONIFEROUS
☐ TROPICAL	☐ OTHER

CAP CHARACTERISTICS
CAP COLOR
CAP SHAPE
CAP TEXTURE
CAP DIAMETER
CAP LENGTH
HYMENIUM
SPECIAL PROPERTIES

STALK CHARACTERISTICS
STALK COLOR
STALK SHAPE
STALK TEXTURE
STALK DIAMETER
STALK LENGTH
STALK SURFACE
SPECIAL PROPERTIES

SURROUNDING PLANTS

FAUNA / WILDLIFE

ADDITIONAL NOTES

DATE	
LOCATION	
GPS	

WEATHER CONDITIONS

SPECIES / TYPE	
SPECIMEN #	
TOTAL LENGTH	

TYPE OF FOREST

- [ ] DECIDUOUS
- [ ] CONIFEROUS
- [ ] TROPICAL
- [ ] OTHER

CAP CHARACTERISTICS

CAP COLOR	
CAP SHAPE	
CAP TEXTURE	
CAP DIAMETER	
CAP LENGTH	
HYMENIUM	
SPECIAL PROPERTIES	

STALK CHARACTERISTICS

STALK COLOR	
STALK SHAPE	
STALK TEXTURE	
STALK DIAMETER	
STALK LENGTH	
STALK SURFACE	
SPECIAL PROPERTIES	

SURROUNDING PLANTS

FAUNA / WILDLIFE

ADDITIONAL NOTES

DATE

LOCATION

GPS

WEATHER CONDITIONS

- [ ] Sunny
- [ ] Partly cloudy
- [ ] Rain
- [ ] Storm
- [ ] Snow

SPECIES / TYPE

SPECIMEN #

TOTAL LENGTH

TYPE OF FOREST

☐ DECIDUOUS	☐ CONIFEROUS
☐ TROPICAL	☐ OTHER

CAP CHARACTERISTICS

CAP COLOR

CAP SHAPE

CAP TEXTURE

CAP DIAMETER

CAP LENGTH

HYMENIUM

SPECIAL PROPERTIES

STALK CHARACTERISTICS

STALK COLOR

STALK SHAPE

STALK TEXTURE

STALK DIAMETER

STALK LENGTH

STALK SURFACE

SPECIAL PROPERTIES

SURROUNDING PLANTS

FAUNA / WILDLIFE

ADDITIONAL NOTES

DATE

LOCATION

GPS

WEATHER CONDITIONS

SPECIES / TYPE

SPECIMEN #

TOTAL LENGTH

TYPE OF FOREST

DECIDUOUS

CONIFEROUS

TROPICAL

OTHER

CAP CHARACTERISTICS

CAP COLOR

CAP SHAPE

CAP TEXTURE

CAP DIAMETER

CAP LENGTH

HYMENIUM

SPECIAL PROPERTIES

STALK CHARACTERISTICS

STALK COLOR

STALK SHAPE

STALK TEXTURE

STALK DIAMETER

STALK LENGTH

STALK SURFACE

SPECIAL PROPERTIES

SURROUNDING PLANTS

FAUNA / WILDLIFE

ADDITIONAL NOTES

DATE
LOCATION
GPS

WEATHER CONDITIONS						
Temperature	____	☐	☐	☐	☐	☐
Wind	____					

SPECIES / TYPE
SPECIMEN #
TOTAL LENGTH

TYPE OF FOREST	
☐ DECIDUOUS	☐ CONIFEROUS
☐ TROPICAL	☐ OTHER

CAP CHARACTERISTICS
CAP COLOR
CAP SHAPE
CAP TEXTURE
CAP DIAMETER
CAP LENGTH
HYMENIUM
SPECIAL PROPERTIES

STALK CHARACTERISTICS
STALK COLOR
STALK SHAPE
STALK TEXTURE
STALK DIAMETER
STALK LENGTH
STALK SURFACE
SPECIAL PROPERTIES

SURROUNDING PLANTS

FAUNA / WILDLIFE

ADDITIONAL NOTES

DATE

LOCATION

GPS

WEATHER CONDITIONS

SPECIES / TYPE

SPECIMEN #

TOTAL LENGTH

TYPE OF FOREST

☐ DECIDUOUS	☐ CONIFEROUS
☐ TROPICAL	☐ OTHER

CAP CHARACTERISTICS

- CAP COLOR
- CAP SHAPE
- CAP TEXTURE
- CAP DIAMETER
- CAP LENGTH
- HYMENIUM
- SPECIAL PROPERTIES

STALK CHARACTERISTICS

- STALK COLOR
- STALK SHAPE
- STALK TEXTURE
- STALK DIAMETER
- STALK LENGTH
- STALK SURFACE
- SPECIAL PROPERTIES

SURROUNDING PLANTS

FAUNA / WILDLIFE

ADDITIONAL NOTES

DATE	
LOCATION	
GPS	

WEATHER CONDITIONS						
Temperature	___	Sunny	Partly cloudy	Rain	Storm	Snow
Wind	___	☐	☐	☐	☐	☐

SPECIES / TYPE	
SPECIMEN #	
TOTAL LENGTH	

TYPE OF FOREST	
☐ DECIDUOUS	☐ CONIFEROUS
☐ TROPICAL	☐ OTHER

CAP CHARACTERISTICS	
CAP COLOR	
CAP SHAPE	
CAP TEXTURE	
CAP DIAMETER	
CAP LENGTH	
HYMENIUM	
SPECIAL PROPERTIES	

STALK CHARACTERISTICS	
STALK COLOR	
STALK SHAPE	
STALK TEXTURE	
STALK DIAMETER	
STALK LENGTH	
STALK SURFACE	
SPECIAL PROPERTIES	

SURROUNDING PLANTS

FAUNA / WILDLIFE

ADDITIONAL NOTES

DATE

LOCATION

GPS

WEATHER CONDITIONS

SPECIES / TYPE

SPECIMEN #

TOTAL LENGTH

TYPE OF FOREST

- [ ] DECIDUOUS
- [ ] CONIFEROUS
- [ ] TROPICAL
- [ ] OTHER

CAP CHARACTERISTICS

CAP COLOR

CAP SHAPE

CAP TEXTURE

CAP DIAMETER

CAP LENGTH

HYMENIUM

SPECIAL PROPERTIES

STALK CHARACTERISTICS

STALK COLOR

STALK SHAPE

STALK TEXTURE

STALK DIAMETER

STALK LENGTH

STALK SURFACE

SPECIAL PROPERTIES

SURROUNDING PLANTS

FAUNA / WILDLIFE

ADDITIONAL NOTES

DATE
LOCATION
GPS

WEATHER CONDITIONS
___ ☐ ☐ ☐ ☐ ☐
___

SPECIES / TYPE
SPECIMEN #
TOTAL LENGTH

TYPE OF FOREST	
☐ DECIDUOUS	☐ CONIFEROUS
☐ TROPICAL	☐ OTHER

CAP CHARACTERISTICS
CAP COLOR
CAP SHAPE
CAP TEXTURE
CAP DIAMETER
CAP LENGTH
HYMENIUM
SPECIAL PROPERTIES

STALK CHARACTERISTICS
STALK COLOR
STALK SHAPE
STALK TEXTURE
STALK DIAMETER
STALK LENGTH
STALK SURFACE
SPECIAL PROPERTIES

SURROUNDING PLANTS

FAUNA / WILDLIFE

ADDITIONAL NOTES

DATE

LOCATION

GPS

WEATHER CONDITIONS

Temperature	____	☐	☐	☐	☐	☐
Wind	____					

SPECIES / TYPE

SPECIMEN #

TOTAL LENGTH

TYPE OF FOREST

☐ DECIDUOUS	☐ CONIFEROUS
☐ TROPICAL	☐ OTHER

CAP CHARACTERISTICS

CAP COLOR

CAP SHAPE

CAP TEXTURE

CAP DIAMETER

CAP LENGTH

HYMENIUM

SPECIAL PROPERTIES

STALK CHARACTERISTICS

STALK COLOR

STALK SHAPE

STALK TEXTURE

STALK DIAMETER

STALK LENGTH

STALK SURFACE

SPECIAL PROPERTIES

SURROUNDING PLANTS

FAUNA / WILDLIFE

ADDITIONAL NOTES

DATE
LOCATION
GPS

WEATHER CONDITIONS
___ ☐ ☐ ☐ ☐ ☐

SPECIES / TYPE
SPECIMEN #
TOTAL LENGTH

TYPE OF FOREST	
☐ DECIDUOUS	☐ CONIFEROUS
☐ TROPICAL	☐ OTHER

CAP CHARACTERISTICS
CAP COLOR
CAP SHAPE
CAP TEXTURE
CAP DIAMETER
CAP LENGTH
HYMENIUM
SPECIAL PROPERTIES

STALK CHARACTERISTICS
STALK COLOR
STALK SHAPE
STALK TEXTURE
STALK DIAMETER
STALK LENGTH
STALK SURFACE
SPECIAL PROPERTIES

SURROUNDING PLANTS

FAUNA / WILDLIFE

ADDITIONAL NOTES

DATE

LOCATION

GPS

WEATHER CONDITIONS

SPECIES / TYPE

SPECIMEN #

TOTAL LENGTH

TYPE OF FOREST

- [ ] DECIDUOUS
- [ ] CONIFEROUS
- [ ] TROPICAL
- [ ] OTHER

CAP CHARACTERISTICS

CAP COLOR

CAP SHAPE

CAP TEXTURE

CAP DIAMETER

CAP LENGTH

HYMENIUM

SPECIAL PROPERTIES

STALK CHARACTERISTICS

STALK COLOR

STALK SHAPE

STALK TEXTURE

STALK DIAMETER

STALK LENGTH

STALK SURFACE

SPECIAL PROPERTIES

SURROUNDING PLANTS

FAUNA / WILDLIFE

ADDITIONAL NOTES

DATE	WEATHER CONDITIONS
LOCATION	
GPS	

SPECIES / TYPE	TYPE OF FOREST	
SPECIMEN #	☐ DECIDUOUS	☐ CONIFEROUS
TOTAL LENGTH	☐ TROPICAL	☐ OTHER

CAP CHARACTERISTICS	STALK CHARACTERISTICS
CAP COLOR	STALK COLOR
CAP SHAPE	STALK SHAPE
CAP TEXTURE	STALK TEXTURE
CAP DIAMETER	STALK DIAMETER
CAP LENGTH	STALK LENGTH
HYMENIUM	STALK SURFACE
SPECIAL PROPERTIES	SPECIAL PROPERTIES

SURROUNDING PLANTS	FAUNA / WILDLIFE

ADDITIONAL NOTES

DATE
LOCATION
GPS

WEATHER CONDITIONS
___
___ ☐ ☐ ☐ ☐ ☐

SPECIES / TYPE
SPECIMEN #
TOTAL LENGTH

TYPE OF FOREST	
☐ DECIDUOUS	☐ CONIFEROUS
☐ TROPICAL	☐ OTHER

CAP CHARACTERISTICS
CAP COLOR
CAP SHAPE
CAP TEXTURE
CAP DIAMETER
CAP LENGTH
HYMENIUM
SPECIAL PROPERTIES

STALK CHARACTERISTICS
STALK COLOR
STALK SHAPE
STALK TEXTURE
STALK DIAMETER
STALK LENGTH
STALK SURFACE
SPECIAL PROPERTIES

SURROUNDING PLANTS

FAUNA / WILDLIFE

ADDITIONAL NOTES

DATE	
LOCATION	
GPS	

WEATHER CONDITIONS						
Temperature	___	☐	☐	☐	☐	☐
Wind	___					

SPECIES / TYPE	
SPECIMEN #	
TOTAL LENGTH	

TYPE OF FOREST	
☐ DECIDUOUS	☐ CONIFEROUS
☐ TROPICAL	☐ OTHER

CAP CHARACTERISTICS	
CAP COLOR	
CAP SHAPE	
CAP TEXTURE	
CAP DIAMETER	
CAP LENGTH	
HYMENIUM	
SPECIAL PROPERTIES	

STALK CHARACTERISTICS	
STALK COLOR	
STALK SHAPE	
STALK TEXTURE	
STALK DIAMETER	
STALK LENGTH	
STALK SURFACE	
SPECIAL PROPERTIES	

SURROUNDING PLANTS

FAUNA / WILDLIFE

ADDITIONAL NOTES

DATE

LOCATION

GPS

WEATHER CONDITIONS

SPECIES / TYPE

SPECIMEN #

TOTAL LENGTH

TYPE OF FOREST

- [ ] DECIDUOUS
- [ ] CONIFEROUS
- [ ] TROPICAL
- [ ] OTHER

CAP CHARACTERISTICS

CAP COLOR

CAP SHAPE

CAP TEXTURE

CAP DIAMETER

CAP LENGTH

HYMENIUM

SPECIAL PROPERTIES

STALK CHARACTERISTICS

STALK COLOR

STALK SHAPE

STALK TEXTURE

STALK DIAMETER

STALK LENGTH

STALK SURFACE

SPECIAL PROPERTIES

SURROUNDING PLANTS

FAUNA / WILDLIFE

ADDITIONAL NOTES

DATE

LOCATION

GPS

WEATHER CONDITIONS

SPECIES / TYPE

SPECIMEN #

TOTAL LENGTH

TYPE OF FOREST

- [ ] DECIDUOUS
- [ ] CONIFEROUS
- [ ] TROPICAL
- [ ] OTHER

CAP CHARACTERISTICS

CAP COLOR

CAP SHAPE

CAP TEXTURE

CAP DIAMETER

CAP LENGTH

HYMENIUM

SPECIAL PROPERTIES

STALK CHARACTERISTICS

STALK COLOR

STALK SHAPE

STALK TEXTURE

STALK DIAMETER

STALK LENGTH

STALK SURFACE

SPECIAL PROPERTIES

SURROUNDING PLANTS

FAUNA / WILDLIFE

ADDITIONAL NOTES

DATE
LOCATION
GPS

WEATHER CONDITIONS
___
___

SPECIES / TYPE
SPECIMEN #
TOTAL LENGTH

TYPE OF FOREST	
☐ DECIDUOUS	☐ CONIFEROUS
☐ TROPICAL	☐ OTHER

CAP CHARACTERISTICS
CAP COLOR
CAP SHAPE
CAP TEXTURE
CAP DIAMETER
CAP LENGTH
HYMENIUM
SPECIAL PROPERTIES

STALK CHARACTERISTICS
STALK COLOR
STALK SHAPE
STALK TEXTURE
STALK DIAMETER
STALK LENGTH
STALK SURFACE
SPECIAL PROPERTIES

SURROUNDING PLANTS

FAUNA / WILDLIFE

ADDITIONAL NOTES

DATE	WEATHER CONDITIONS
LOCATION	
GPS	

SPECIES / TYPE	TYPE OF FOREST	
SPECIMEN #	☐ DECIDUOUS	☐ CONIFEROUS
TOTAL LENGTH	☐ TROPICAL	☐ OTHER

CAP CHARACTERISTICS	STALK CHARACTERISTICS
CAP COLOR	STALK COLOR
CAP SHAPE	STALK SHAPE
CAP TEXTURE	STALK TEXTURE
CAP DIAMETER	STALK DIAMETER
CAP LENGTH	STALK LENGTH
HYMENIUM	STALK SURFACE
SPECIAL PROPERTIES	SPECIAL PROPERTIES

SURROUNDING PLANTS	FAUNA / WILDLIFE

ADDITIONAL NOTES

DATE

LOCATION

GPS

WEATHER CONDITIONS

SPECIES / TYPE

SPECIMEN #

TOTAL LENGTH

TYPE OF FOREST

DECIDUOUS

CONIFEROUS

TROPICAL

OTHER

CAP CHARACTERISTICS

CAP COLOR

CAP SHAPE

CAP TEXTURE

CAP DIAMETER

CAP LENGTH

HYMENIUM

SPECIAL PROPERTIES

STALK CHARACTERISTICS

STALK COLOR

STALK SHAPE

STALK TEXTURE

STALK DIAMETER

STALK LENGTH

STALK SURFACE

SPECIAL PROPERTIES

SURROUNDING PLANTS

FAUNA / WILDLIFE

ADDITIONAL NOTES

DATE
LOCATION
GPS

WEATHER CONDITIONS

SPECIES / TYPE
SPECIMEN #
TOTAL LENGTH

TYPE OF FOREST	
☐ DECIDUOUS	☐ CONIFEROUS
☐ TROPICAL	☐ OTHER

CAP CHARACTERISTICS
CAP COLOR
CAP SHAPE
CAP TEXTURE
CAP DIAMETER
CAP LENGTH
HYMENIUM
SPECIAL PROPERTIES

STALK CHARACTERISTICS
STALK COLOR
STALK SHAPE
STALK TEXTURE
STALK DIAMETER
STALK LENGTH
STALK SURFACE
SPECIAL PROPERTIES

SURROUNDING PLANTS

FAUNA / WILDLIFE

ADDITIONAL NOTES

DATE
LOCATION
GPS

WEATHER CONDITIONS

SPECIES / TYPE
SPECIMEN #
TOTAL LENGTH

TYPE OF FOREST	
☐ DECIDUOUS	☐ CONIFEROUS
☐ TROPICAL	☐ OTHER

CAP CHARACTERISTICS
CAP COLOR
CAP SHAPE
CAP TEXTURE
CAP DIAMETER
CAP LENGTH
HYMENIUM
SPECIAL PROPERTIES

STALK CHARACTERISTICS
STALK COLOR
STALK SHAPE
STALK TEXTURE
STALK DIAMETER
STALK LENGTH
STALK SURFACE
SPECIAL PROPERTIES

SURROUNDING PLANTS

FAUNA / WILDLIFE

ADDITIONAL NOTES

DATE	
LOCATION	
GPS	

WEATHER CONDITIONS
Temperature ____ ☐ ☐ ☐ ☐ ☐
Wind ____

SPECIES / TYPE	
SPECIMEN #	
TOTAL LENGTH	

TYPE OF FOREST	
☐ DECIDUOUS	☐ CONIFEROUS
☐ TROPICAL	☐ OTHER

CAP CHARACTERISTICS	
CAP COLOR	
CAP SHAPE	
CAP TEXTURE	
CAP DIAMETER	
CAP LENGTH	
HYMENIUM	
SPECIAL PROPERTIES	

STALK CHARACTERISTICS	
STALK COLOR	
STALK SHAPE	
STALK TEXTURE	
STALK DIAMETER	
STALK LENGTH	
STALK SURFACE	
SPECIAL PROPERTIES	

SURROUNDING PLANTS

FAUNA / WILDLIFE

ADDITIONAL NOTES

DATE
LOCATION
GPS

WEATHER CONDITIONS

SPECIES / TYPE
SPECIMEN #
TOTAL LENGTH

TYPE OF FOREST	
☐ DECIDUOUS	☐ CONIFEROUS
☐ TROPICAL	☐ OTHER

CAP CHARACTERISTICS
CAP COLOR
CAP SHAPE
CAP TEXTURE
CAP DIAMETER
CAP LENGTH
HYMENIUM
SPECIAL PROPERTIES

STALK CHARACTERISTICS
STALK COLOR
STALK SHAPE
STALK TEXTURE
STALK DIAMETER
STALK LENGTH
STALK SURFACE
SPECIAL PROPERTIES

SURROUNDING PLANTS

FAUNA / WILDLIFE

ADDITIONAL NOTES

DATE

LOCATION

GPS

WEATHER CONDITIONS

SPECIES / TYPE

SPECIMEN #

TOTAL LENGTH

TYPE OF FOREST

DECIDUOUS	CONIFEROUS
TROPICAL	OTHER

CAP CHARACTERISTICS

CAP COLOR

CAP SHAPE

CAP TEXTURE

CAP DIAMETER

CAP LENGTH

HYMENIUM

SPECIAL PROPERTIES

STALK CHARACTERISTICS

STALK COLOR

STALK SHAPE

STALK TEXTURE

STALK DIAMETER

STALK LENGTH

STALK SURFACE

SPECIAL PROPERTIES

SURROUNDING PLANTS

FAUNA / WILDLIFE

ADDITIONAL NOTES

DATE

LOCATION

GPS

WEATHER CONDITIONS

SPECIES / TYPE

SPECIMEN #

TOTAL LENGTH

TYPE OF FOREST

DECIDUOUS	CONIFEROUS
TROPICAL	OTHER

CAP CHARACTERISTICS

CAP COLOR

CAP SHAPE

CAP TEXTURE

CAP DIAMETER

CAP LENGTH

HYMENIUM

SPECIAL PROPERTIES

STALK CHARACTERISTICS

STALK COLOR

STALK SHAPE

STALK TEXTURE

STALK DIAMETER

STALK LENGTH

STALK SURFACE

SPECIAL PROPERTIES

SURROUNDING PLANTS

FAUNA / WILDLIFE

ADDITIONAL NOTES

DATE
LOCATION
GPS

WEATHER CONDITIONS

SPECIES / TYPE
SPECIMEN #
TOTAL LENGTH

TYPE OF FOREST	
☐ DECIDUOUS	☐ CONIFEROUS
☐ TROPICAL	☐ OTHER

CAP CHARACTERISTICS
CAP COLOR
CAP SHAPE
CAP TEXTURE
CAP DIAMETER
CAP LENGTH
HYMENIUM
SPECIAL PROPERTIES

STALK CHARACTERISTICS
STALK COLOR
STALK SHAPE
STALK TEXTURE
STALK DIAMETER
STALK LENGTH
STALK SURFACE
SPECIAL PROPERTIES

SURROUNDING PLANTS

FAUNA / WILDLIFE

ADDITIONAL NOTES

DATE

LOCATION

GPS

WEATHER CONDITIONS

SPECIES / TYPE

SPECIMEN #

TOTAL LENGTH

TYPE OF FOREST

☐ DECIDUOUS	☐ CONIFEROUS
☐ TROPICAL	☐ OTHER

CAP CHARACTERISTICS

CAP COLOR

CAP SHAPE

CAP TEXTURE

CAP DIAMETER

CAP LENGTH

HYMENIUM

SPECIAL PROPERTIES

STALK CHARACTERISTICS

STALK COLOR

STALK SHAPE

STALK TEXTURE

STALK DIAMETER

STALK LENGTH

STALK SURFACE

SPECIAL PROPERTIES

SURROUNDING PLANTS

FAUNA / WILDLIFE

ADDITIONAL NOTES

DATE

LOCATION

GPS

WEATHER CONDITIONS

SPECIES / TYPE

SPECIMEN #

TOTAL LENGTH

TYPE OF FOREST

- [ ] DECIDUOUS
- [ ] CONIFEROUS
- [ ] TROPICAL
- [ ] OTHER

CAP CHARACTERISTICS

CAP COLOR

CAP SHAPE

CAP TEXTURE

CAP DIAMETER

CAP LENGTH

HYMENIUM

SPECIAL PROPERTIES

STALK CHARACTERISTICS

STALK COLOR

STALK SHAPE

STALK TEXTURE

STALK DIAMETER

STALK LENGTH

STALK SURFACE

SPECIAL PROPERTIES

SURROUNDING PLANTS

FAUNA / WILDLIFE

ADDITIONAL NOTES

DATE

LOCATION

GPS

WEATHER CONDITIONS

SPECIES / TYPE

SPECIMEN #

TOTAL LENGTH

TYPE OF FOREST

- [ ] DECIDUOUS
- [ ] CONIFEROUS
- [ ] TROPICAL
- [ ] OTHER

CAP CHARACTERISTICS

CAP COLOR

CAP SHAPE

CAP TEXTURE

CAP DIAMETER

CAP LENGTH

HYMENIUM

SPECIAL PROPERTIES

STALK CHARACTERISTICS

STALK COLOR

STALK SHAPE

STALK TEXTURE

STALK DIAMETER

STALK LENGTH

STALK SURFACE

SPECIAL PROPERTIES

SURROUNDING PLANTS

FAUNA / WILDLIFE

ADDITIONAL NOTES

DATE	WEATHER CONDITIONS
LOCATION	
GPS	

SPECIES / TYPE
SPECIMEN #
TOTAL LENGTH

TYPE OF FOREST	
☐ DECIDUOUS	☐ CONIFEROUS
☐ TROPICAL	☐ OTHER

CAP CHARACTERISTICS	STALK CHARACTERISTICS
CAP COLOR	STALK COLOR
CAP SHAPE	STALK SHAPE
CAP TEXTURE	STALK TEXTURE
CAP DIAMETER	STALK DIAMETER
CAP LENGTH	STALK LENGTH
HYMENIUM	STALK SURFACE
SPECIAL PROPERTIES	SPECIAL PROPERTIES

SURROUNDING PLANTS	FAUNA / WILDLIFE

ADDITIONAL NOTES

DATE
LOCATION
GPS

WEATHER CONDITIONS
____ ☐ ☐ ☐ ☐ ☐
____

SPECIES / TYPE
SPECIMEN #
TOTAL LENGTH

TYPE OF FOREST	
☐ DECIDUOUS	☐ CONIFEROUS
☐ TROPICAL	☐ OTHER

CAP CHARACTERISTICS
CAP COLOR
CAP SHAPE
CAP TEXTURE
CAP DIAMETER
CAP LENGTH
HYMENIUM
SPECIAL PROPERTIES

STALK CHARACTERISTICS
STALK COLOR
STALK SHAPE
STALK TEXTURE
STALK DIAMETER
STALK LENGTH
STALK SURFACE
SPECIAL PROPERTIES

SURROUNDING PLANTS

FAUNA / WILDLIFE

ADDITIONAL NOTES

DATE
LOCATION
GPS

WEATHER CONDITIONS
___ ☐ ☐ ☐ ☐ ☐
___

SPECIES / TYPE
SPECIMEN #
TOTAL LENGTH

TYPE OF FOREST	
☐ DECIDUOUS	☐ CONIFEROUS
☐ TROPICAL	☐ OTHER

CAP CHARACTERISTICS
CAP COLOR
CAP SHAPE
CAP TEXTURE
CAP DIAMETER
CAP LENGTH
HYMENIUM
SPECIAL PROPERTIES

STALK CHARACTERISTICS
STALK COLOR
STALK SHAPE
STALK TEXTURE
STALK DIAMETER
STALK LENGTH
STALK SURFACE
SPECIAL PROPERTIES

SURROUNDING PLANTS

FAUNA / WILDLIFE

ADDITIONAL NOTES

DATE
LOCATION
GPS

WEATHER CONDITIONS
___ ☐ ☐ ☐ ☐ ☐
___

SPECIES / TYPE
SPECIMEN #
TOTAL LENGTH

TYPE OF FOREST	
☐ DECIDUOUS	☐ CONIFEROUS
☐ TROPICAL	☐ OTHER

CAP CHARACTERISTICS
CAP COLOR
CAP SHAPE
CAP TEXTURE
CAP DIAMETER
CAP LENGTH
HYMENIUM
SPECIAL PROPERTIES

STALK CHARACTERISTICS
STALK COLOR
STALK SHAPE
STALK TEXTURE
STALK DIAMETER
STALK LENGTH
STALK SURFACE
SPECIAL PROPERTIES

SURROUNDING PLANTS

FAUNA / WILDLIFE

ADDITIONAL NOTES

DATE
LOCATION
GPS

WEATHER CONDITIONS

	____	☐	☐	☐	☐	☐
	____	☐	☐	☐	☐	☐

SPECIES / TYPE
SPECIMEN #
TOTAL LENGTH

TYPE OF FOREST

☐ DECIDUOUS	☐ CONIFEROUS
☐ TROPICAL	☐ OTHER

CAP CHARACTERISTICS

- CAP COLOR
- CAP SHAPE
- CAP TEXTURE
- CAP DIAMETER
- CAP LENGTH
- HYMENIUM
- SPECIAL PROPERTIES

STALK CHARACTERISTICS

- STALK COLOR
- STALK SHAPE
- STALK TEXTURE
- STALK DIAMETER
- STALK LENGTH
- STALK SURFACE
- SPECIAL PROPERTIES

SURROUNDING PLANTS

FAUNA / WILDLIFE

ADDITIONAL NOTES

DATE
LOCATION
GPS

WEATHER CONDITIONS
☐ ☐ ☐ ☐ ☐

SPECIES / TYPE
SPECIMEN #
TOTAL LENGTH

TYPE OF FOREST	
☐ DECIDUOUS	☐ CONIFEROUS
☐ TROPICAL	☐ OTHER

CAP CHARACTERISTICS
CAP COLOR
CAP SHAPE
CAP TEXTURE
CAP DIAMETER
CAP LENGTH
HYMENIUM
SPECIAL PROPERTIES

STALK CHARACTERISTICS
STALK COLOR
STALK SHAPE
STALK TEXTURE
STALK DIAMETER
STALK LENGTH
STALK SURFACE
SPECIAL PROPERTIES

SURROUNDING PLANTS

FAUNA / WILDLIFE

ADDITIONAL NOTES

DATE
LOCATION
GPS

WEATHER CONDITIONS

SPECIES / TYPE
SPECIMEN #
TOTAL LENGTH

TYPE OF FOREST	
☐ DECIDUOUS	☐ CONIFEROUS
☐ TROPICAL	☐ OTHER

CAP CHARACTERISTICS
CAP COLOR
CAP SHAPE
CAP TEXTURE
CAP DIAMETER
CAP LENGTH
HYMENIUM
SPECIAL PROPERTIES

STALK CHARACTERISTICS
STALK COLOR
STALK SHAPE
STALK TEXTURE
STALK DIAMETER
STALK LENGTH
STALK SURFACE
SPECIAL PROPERTIES

SURROUNDING PLANTS

FAUNA / WILDLIFE

ADDITIONAL NOTES

DATE	
LOCATION	
GPS	

WEATHER CONDITIONS

SPECIES / TYPE	
SPECIMEN #	
TOTAL LENGTH	

TYPE OF FOREST	
☐ DECIDUOUS	☐ CONIFEROUS
☐ TROPICAL	☐ OTHER

CAP CHARACTERISTICS	
CAP COLOR	
CAP SHAPE	
CAP TEXTURE	
CAP DIAMETER	
CAP LENGTH	
HYMENIUM	
SPECIAL PROPERTIES	

STALK CHARACTERISTICS	
STALK COLOR	
STALK SHAPE	
STALK TEXTURE	
STALK DIAMETER	
STALK LENGTH	
STALK SURFACE	
SPECIAL PROPERTIES	

SURROUNDING PLANTS

FAUNA / WILDLIFE

ADDITIONAL NOTES

DATE	
LOCATION	
GPS	

WEATHER CONDITIONS

SPECIES / TYPE	
SPECIMEN #	
TOTAL LENGTH	

TYPE OF FOREST	
☐ DECIDUOUS	☐ CONIFEROUS
☐ TROPICAL	☐ OTHER

CAP CHARACTERISTICS	
CAP COLOR	
CAP SHAPE	
CAP TEXTURE	
CAP DIAMETER	
CAP LENGTH	
HYMENIUM	
SPECIAL PROPERTIES	

STALK CHARACTERISTICS	
STALK COLOR	
STALK SHAPE	
STALK TEXTURE	
STALK DIAMETER	
STALK LENGTH	
STALK SURFACE	
SPECIAL PROPERTIES	

SURROUNDING PLANTS

FAUNA / WILDLIFE

ADDITIONAL NOTES

DATE

LOCATION

GPS

WEATHER CONDITIONS

- [ ] ☀
- [ ] ⛅
- [ ] 🌧
- [ ] ⛈
- [ ] ❄

SPECIES / TYPE

SPECIMEN #

TOTAL LENGTH

TYPE OF FOREST

- [ ] DECIDUOUS
- [ ] CONIFEROUS
- [ ] TROPICAL
- [ ] OTHER

CAP CHARACTERISTICS

CAP COLOR

CAP SHAPE

CAP TEXTURE

CAP DIAMETER

CAP LENGTH

HYMENIUM

SPECIAL PROPERTIES

STALK CHARACTERISTICS

STALK COLOR

STALK SHAPE

STALK TEXTURE

STALK DIAMETER

STALK LENGTH

STALK SURFACE

SPECIAL PROPERTIES

SURROUNDING PLANTS

FAUNA / WILDLIFE

ADDITIONAL NOTES

DATE

LOCATION

GPS

WEATHER CONDITIONS

SPECIES / TYPE

SPECIMEN #

TOTAL LENGTH

TYPE OF FOREST

- [ ] DECIDUOUS
- [ ] CONIFEROUS
- [ ] TROPICAL
- [ ] OTHER

CAP CHARACTERISTICS

CAP COLOR

CAP SHAPE

CAP TEXTURE

CAP DIAMETER

CAP LENGTH

HYMENIUM

SPECIAL PROPERTIES

STALK CHARACTERISTICS

STALK COLOR

STALK SHAPE

STALK TEXTURE

STALK DIAMETER

STALK LENGTH

STALK SURFACE

SPECIAL PROPERTIES

SURROUNDING PLANTS

FAUNA / WILDLIFE

ADDITIONAL NOTES

DATE
LOCATION
GPS

WEATHER CONDITIONS

SPECIES / TYPE
SPECIMEN #
TOTAL LENGTH

TYPE OF FOREST	
☐ DECIDUOUS	☐ CONIFEROUS
☐ TROPICAL	☐ OTHER

CAP CHARACTERISTICS
CAP COLOR
CAP SHAPE
CAP TEXTURE
CAP DIAMETER
CAP LENGTH
HYMENIUM
SPECIAL PROPERTIES

STALK CHARACTERISTICS
STALK COLOR
STALK SHAPE
STALK TEXTURE
STALK DIAMETER
STALK LENGTH
STALK SURFACE
SPECIAL PROPERTIES

SURROUNDING PLANTS

FAUNA / WILDLIFE

ADDITIONAL NOTES

DATE	
LOCATION	
GPS	

WEATHER CONDITIONS					
___	☐	☐	☐	☐	☐
___					

SPECIES / TYPE	
SPECIMEN #	
TOTAL LENGTH	

TYPE OF FOREST	
☐ DECIDUOUS	☐ CONIFEROUS
☐ TROPICAL	☐ OTHER

CAP CHARACTERISTICS	
CAP COLOR	
CAP SHAPE	
CAP TEXTURE	
CAP DIAMETER	
CAP LENGTH	
HYMENIUM	
SPECIAL PROPERTIES	

STALK CHARACTERISTICS	
STALK COLOR	
STALK SHAPE	
STALK TEXTURE	
STALK DIAMETER	
STALK LENGTH	
STALK SURFACE	
SPECIAL PROPERTIES	

SURROUNDING PLANTS

FAUNA / WILDLIFE

ADDITIONAL NOTES

DATE

LOCATION

GPS

WEATHER CONDITIONS

SPECIES / TYPE

SPECIMEN #

TOTAL LENGTH

TYPE OF FOREST

- [ ] DECIDUOUS
- [ ] CONIFEROUS
- [ ] TROPICAL
- [ ] OTHER

CAP CHARACTERISTICS

CAP COLOR

CAP SHAPE

CAP TEXTURE

CAP DIAMETER

CAP LENGTH

HYMENIUM

SPECIAL PROPERTIES

STALK CHARACTERISTICS

STALK COLOR

STALK SHAPE

STALK TEXTURE

STALK DIAMETER

STALK LENGTH

STALK SURFACE

SPECIAL PROPERTIES

SURROUNDING PLANTS

FAUNA / WILDLIFE

ADDITIONAL NOTES

DATE
LOCATION
GPS

WEATHER CONDITIONS

SPECIES / TYPE
SPECIMEN #
TOTAL LENGTH

TYPE OF FOREST	
☐ DECIDUOUS	☐ CONIFEROUS
☐ TROPICAL	☐ OTHER

CAP CHARACTERISTICS
CAP COLOR
CAP SHAPE
CAP TEXTURE
CAP DIAMETER
CAP LENGTH
HYMENIUM
SPECIAL PROPERTIES

STALK CHARACTERISTICS
STALK COLOR
STALK SHAPE
STALK TEXTURE
STALK DIAMETER
STALK LENGTH
STALK SURFACE
SPECIAL PROPERTIES

SURROUNDING PLANTS

FAUNA / WILDLIFE

ADDITIONAL NOTES

DATE	
LOCATION	
GPS	

WEATHER CONDITIONS						
Temperature	____	☐	☐	☐	☐	☐
Wind	____					

SPECIES / TYPE	
SPECIMEN #	
TOTAL LENGTH	

TYPE OF FOREST	
☐ DECIDUOUS	☐ CONIFEROUS
☐ TROPICAL	☐ OTHER

CAP CHARACTERISTICS	
CAP COLOR	
CAP SHAPE	
CAP TEXTURE	
CAP DIAMETER	
CAP LENGTH	
HYMENIUM	
SPECIAL PROPERTIES	

STALK CHARACTERISTICS	
STALK COLOR	
STALK SHAPE	
STALK TEXTURE	
STALK DIAMETER	
STALK LENGTH	
STALK SURFACE	
SPECIAL PROPERTIES	

SURROUNDING PLANTS

FAUNA / WILDLIFE

ADDITIONAL NOTES

DATE

LOCATION

GPS

WEATHER CONDITIONS

SPECIES / TYPE

SPECIMEN #

TOTAL LENGTH

TYPE OF FOREST

☐ DECIDUOUS	☐ CONIFEROUS
☐ TROPICAL	☐ OTHER

CAP CHARACTERISTICS

CAP COLOR

CAP SHAPE

CAP TEXTURE

CAP DIAMETER

CAP LENGTH

HYMENIUM

SPECIAL PROPERTIES

STALK CHARACTERISTICS

STALK COLOR

STALK SHAPE

STALK TEXTURE

STALK DIAMETER

STALK LENGTH

STALK SURFACE

SPECIAL PROPERTIES

SURROUNDING PLANTS

FAUNA / WILDLIFE

ADDITIONAL NOTES

DATE

LOCATION

GPS

WEATHER CONDITIONS

SPECIES / TYPE

SPECIMEN #

TOTAL LENGTH

TYPE OF FOREST

- [ ] DECIDUOUS
- [ ] CONIFEROUS
- [ ] TROPICAL
- [ ] OTHER

CAP CHARACTERISTICS

CAP COLOR

CAP SHAPE

CAP TEXTURE

CAP DIAMETER

CAP LENGTH

HYMENIUM

SPECIAL PROPERTIES

STALK CHARACTERISTICS

STALK COLOR

STALK SHAPE

STALK TEXTURE

STALK DIAMETER

STALK LENGTH

STALK SURFACE

SPECIAL PROPERTIES

SURROUNDING PLANTS

FAUNA / WILDLIFE

ADDITIONAL NOTES

DATE	
LOCATION	
GPS	

WEATHER CONDITIONS

SPECIES / TYPE	
SPECIMEN #	
TOTAL LENGTH	

TYPE OF FOREST	
☐ DECIDUOUS	☐ CONIFEROUS
☐ TROPICAL	☐ OTHER

CAP CHARACTERISTICS	
CAP COLOR	
CAP SHAPE	
CAP TEXTURE	
CAP DIAMETER	
CAP LENGTH	
HYMENIUM	
SPECIAL PROPERTIES	

STALK CHARACTERISTICS	
STALK COLOR	
STALK SHAPE	
STALK TEXTURE	
STALK DIAMETER	
STALK LENGTH	
STALK SURFACE	
SPECIAL PROPERTIES	

SURROUNDING PLANTS

FAUNA / WILDLIFE

ADDITIONAL NOTES

DATE

LOCATION

GPS

WEATHER CONDITIONS

SPECIES / TYPE

SPECIMEN #

TOTAL LENGTH

TYPE OF FOREST

☐ DECIDUOUS	☐ CONIFEROUS
☐ TROPICAL	☐ OTHER

CAP CHARACTERISTICS

CAP COLOR

CAP SHAPE

CAP TEXTURE

CAP DIAMETER

CAP LENGTH

HYMENIUM

SPECIAL PROPERTIES

STALK CHARACTERISTICS

STALK COLOR

STALK SHAPE

STALK TEXTURE

STALK DIAMETER

STALK LENGTH

STALK SURFACE

SPECIAL PROPERTIES

SURROUNDING PLANTS

FAUNA / WILDLIFE

ADDITIONAL NOTES

DATE
LOCATION
GPS

WEATHER CONDITIONS

SPECIES / TYPE
SPECIMEN #
TOTAL LENGTH

TYPE OF FOREST	
☐ DECIDUOUS	☐ CONIFEROUS
☐ TROPICAL	☐ OTHER

CAP CHARACTERISTICS
CAP COLOR
CAP SHAPE
CAP TEXTURE
CAP DIAMETER
CAP LENGTH
HYMENIUM
SPECIAL PROPERTIES

STALK CHARACTERISTICS
STALK COLOR
STALK SHAPE
STALK TEXTURE
STALK DIAMETER
STALK LENGTH
STALK SURFACE
SPECIAL PROPERTIES

SURROUNDING PLANTS

FAUNA / WILDLIFE

ADDITIONAL NOTES

DATE

LOCATION

GPS

WEATHER CONDITIONS					
___					
___	☐	☐	☐	☐	☐

SPECIES / TYPE

SPECIMEN #

TOTAL LENGTH

TYPE OF FOREST	
☐ DECIDUOUS	☐ CONIFEROUS
☐ TROPICAL	☐ OTHER

CAP CHARACTERISTICS

CAP COLOR

CAP SHAPE

CAP TEXTURE

CAP DIAMETER

CAP LENGTH

HYMENIUM

SPECIAL PROPERTIES

STALK CHARACTERISTICS

STALK COLOR

STALK SHAPE

STALK TEXTURE

STALK DIAMETER

STALK LENGTH

STALK SURFACE

SPECIAL PROPERTIES

SURROUNDING PLANTS

FAUNA / WILDLIFE

ADDITIONAL NOTES

DATE	
LOCATION	
GPS	

WEATHER CONDITIONS

____	☐	☐	☐	☐	☐

SPECIES / TYPE	
SPECIMEN #	
TOTAL LENGTH	

TYPE OF FOREST

☐ DECIDUOUS	☐ CONIFEROUS
☐ TROPICAL	☐ OTHER

CAP CHARACTERISTICS

CAP COLOR	
CAP SHAPE	
CAP TEXTURE	
CAP DIAMETER	
CAP LENGTH	
HYMENIUM	
SPECIAL PROPERTIES	

STALK CHARACTERISTICS

STALK COLOR	
STALK SHAPE	
STALK TEXTURE	
STALK DIAMETER	
STALK LENGTH	
STALK SURFACE	
SPECIAL PROPERTIES	

SURROUNDING PLANTS

FAUNA / WILDLIFE

ADDITIONAL NOTES

DATE

LOCATION

GPS

WEATHER CONDITIONS

SPECIES / TYPE

SPECIMEN #

TOTAL LENGTH

TYPE OF FOREST

- [ ] DECIDUOUS
- [ ] CONIFEROUS
- [ ] TROPICAL
- [ ] OTHER

CAP CHARACTERISTICS

CAP COLOR

CAP SHAPE

CAP TEXTURE

CAP DIAMETER

CAP LENGTH

HYMENIUM

SPECIAL PROPERTIES

STALK CHARACTERISTICS

STALK COLOR

STALK SHAPE

STALK TEXTURE

STALK DIAMETER

STALK LENGTH

STALK SURFACE

SPECIAL PROPERTIES

SURROUNDING PLANTS

FAUNA / WILDLIFE

ADDITIONAL NOTES

DATE

LOCATION

GPS

WEATHER CONDITIONS

SPECIES / TYPE

SPECIMEN #

TOTAL LENGTH

TYPE OF FOREST

☐ DECIDUOUS	☐ CONIFEROUS
☐ TROPICAL	☐ OTHER

CAP CHARACTERISTICS

- CAP COLOR
- CAP SHAPE
- CAP TEXTURE
- CAP DIAMETER
- CAP LENGTH
- HYMENIUM
- SPECIAL PROPERTIES

STALK CHARACTERISTICS

- STALK COLOR
- STALK SHAPE
- STALK TEXTURE
- STALK DIAMETER
- STALK LENGTH
- STALK SURFACE
- SPECIAL PROPERTIES

SURROUNDING PLANTS

FAUNA / WILDLIFE

ADDITIONAL NOTES

DATE
LOCATION
GPS

WEATHER CONDITIONS

SPECIES / TYPE
SPECIMEN #
TOTAL LENGTH

TYPE OF FOREST	
☐ DECIDUOUS	☐ CONIFEROUS
☐ TROPICAL	☐ OTHER

CAP CHARACTERISTICS
CAP COLOR
CAP SHAPE
CAP TEXTURE
CAP DIAMETER
CAP LENGTH
HYMENIUM
SPECIAL PROPERTIES

STALK CHARACTERISTICS
STALK COLOR
STALK SHAPE
STALK TEXTURE
STALK DIAMETER
STALK LENGTH
STALK SURFACE
SPECIAL PROPERTIES

SURROUNDING PLANTS

FAUNA / WILDLIFE

ADDITIONAL NOTES

DATE
LOCATION
GPS

WEATHER CONDITIONS						
	____					
	____	☐	☐	☐	☐	☐

SPECIES / TYPE
SPECIMEN #
TOTAL LENGTH

TYPE OF FOREST	
☐ DECIDUOUS	☐ CONIFEROUS
☐ TROPICAL	☐ OTHER

CAP CHARACTERISTICS
CAP COLOR
CAP SHAPE
CAP TEXTURE
CAP DIAMETER
CAP LENGTH
HYMENIUM
SPECIAL PROPERTIES

STALK CHARACTERISTICS
STALK COLOR
STALK SHAPE
STALK TEXTURE
STALK DIAMETER
STALK LENGTH
STALK SURFACE
SPECIAL PROPERTIES

SURROUNDING PLANTS

FAUNA / WILDLIFE

ADDITIONAL NOTES

DATE

LOCATION

GPS

WEATHER CONDITIONS

SPECIES / TYPE

SPECIMEN #

TOTAL LENGTH

TYPE OF FOREST

- [ ] DECIDUOUS
- [ ] CONIFEROUS
- [ ] TROPICAL
- [ ] OTHER

CAP CHARACTERISTICS

CAP COLOR

CAP SHAPE

CAP TEXTURE

CAP DIAMETER

CAP LENGTH

HYMENIUM

SPECIAL PROPERTIES

STALK CHARACTERISTICS

STALK COLOR

STALK SHAPE

STALK TEXTURE

STALK DIAMETER

STALK LENGTH

STALK SURFACE

SPECIAL PROPERTIES

SURROUNDING PLANTS

FAUNA / WILDLIFE

ADDITIONAL NOTES

DATE

LOCATION

GPS

WEATHER CONDITIONS

SPECIES / TYPE

SPECIMEN #

TOTAL LENGTH

TYPE OF FOREST

☐ DECIDUOUS	☐ CONIFEROUS
☐ TROPICAL	☐ OTHER

CAP CHARACTERISTICS

CAP COLOR

CAP SHAPE

CAP TEXTURE

CAP DIAMETER

CAP LENGTH

HYMENIUM

SPECIAL PROPERTIES

STALK CHARACTERISTICS

STALK COLOR

STALK SHAPE

STALK TEXTURE

STALK DIAMETER

STALK LENGTH

STALK SURFACE

SPECIAL PROPERTIES

SURROUNDING PLANTS

FAUNA / WILDLIFE

ADDITIONAL NOTES

DATE

LOCATION

GPS

WEATHER CONDITIONS

SPECIES / TYPE

SPECIMEN #

TOTAL LENGTH

TYPE OF FOREST

DECIDUOUS	CONIFEROUS
TROPICAL	OTHER

CAP CHARACTERISTICS

CAP COLOR

CAP SHAPE

CAP TEXTURE

CAP DIAMETER

CAP LENGTH

HYMENIUM

SPECIAL PROPERTIES

STALK CHARACTERISTICS

STALK COLOR

STALK SHAPE

STALK TEXTURE

STALK DIAMETER

STALK LENGTH

STALK SURFACE

SPECIAL PROPERTIES

SURROUNDING PLANTS

FAUNA / WILDLIFE

ADDITIONAL NOTES

DATE
LOCATION
GPS

WEATHER CONDITIONS

SPECIES / TYPE
SPECIMEN #
TOTAL LENGTH

TYPE OF FOREST	
☐ DECIDUOUS	☐ CONIFEROUS
☐ TROPICAL	☐ OTHER

CAP CHARACTERISTICS
CAP COLOR
CAP SHAPE
CAP TEXTURE
CAP DIAMETER
CAP LENGTH
HYMENIUM
SPECIAL PROPERTIES

STALK CHARACTERISTICS
STALK COLOR
STALK SHAPE
STALK TEXTURE
STALK DIAMETER
STALK LENGTH
STALK SURFACE
SPECIAL PROPERTIES

SURROUNDING PLANTS

FAUNA / WILDLIFE

ADDITIONAL NOTES

DATE	WEATHER CONDITIONS
LOCATION	
GPS	

SPECIES / TYPE	TYPE OF FOREST	
SPECIMEN #	DECIDUOUS	CONIFEROUS
TOTAL LENGTH	TROPICAL	OTHER

CAP CHARACTERISTICS	STALK CHARACTERISTICS
CAP COLOR	STALK COLOR
CAP SHAPE	STALK SHAPE
CAP TEXTURE	STALK TEXTURE
CAP DIAMETER	STALK DIAMETER
CAP LENGTH	STALK LENGTH
HYMENIUM	STALK SURFACE
SPECIAL PROPERTIES	SPECIAL PROPERTIES

SURROUNDING PLANTS	FAUNA / WILDLIFE

ADDITIONAL NOTES

DATE	
LOCATION	
GPS	

WEATHER CONDITIONS

SPECIES / TYPE	
SPECIMEN #	
TOTAL LENGTH	

TYPE OF FOREST	
☐ DECIDUOUS	☐ CONIFEROUS
☐ TROPICAL	☐ OTHER

CAP CHARACTERISTICS
CAP COLOR
CAP SHAPE
CAP TEXTURE
CAP DIAMETER
CAP LENGTH
HYMENIUM
SPECIAL PROPERTIES

STALK CHARACTERISTICS
STALK COLOR
STALK SHAPE
STALK TEXTURE
STALK DIAMETER
STALK LENGTH
STALK SURFACE
SPECIAL PROPERTIES

SURROUNDING PLANTS

FAUNA / WILDLIFE

ADDITIONAL NOTES

DATE
LOCATION
GPS

WEATHER CONDITIONS

SPECIES / TYPE
SPECIMEN #
TOTAL LENGTH

TYPE OF FOREST	
☐ DECIDUOUS	☐ CONIFEROUS
☐ TROPICAL	☐ OTHER

CAP CHARACTERISTICS
CAP COLOR
CAP SHAPE
CAP TEXTURE
CAP DIAMETER
CAP LENGTH
HYMENIUM
SPECIAL PROPERTIES

STALK CHARACTERISTICS
STALK COLOR
STALK SHAPE
STALK TEXTURE
STALK DIAMETER
STALK LENGTH
STALK SURFACE
SPECIAL PROPERTIES

SURROUNDING PLANTS

FAUNA / WILDLIFE

ADDITIONAL NOTES

DATE	
LOCATION	
GPS	

WEATHER CONDITIONS					
____					
____	☐	☐	☐	☐	☐

SPECIES / TYPE	
SPECIMEN #	
TOTAL LENGTH	

TYPE OF FOREST	
☐ DECIDUOUS	☐ CONIFEROUS
☐ TROPICAL	☐ OTHER

CAP CHARACTERISTICS	
CAP COLOR	
CAP SHAPE	
CAP TEXTURE	
CAP DIAMETER	
CAP LENGTH	
HYMENIUM	
SPECIAL PROPERTIES	

STALK CHARACTERISTICS	
STALK COLOR	
STALK SHAPE	
STALK TEXTURE	
STALK DIAMETER	
STALK LENGTH	
STALK SURFACE	
SPECIAL PROPERTIES	

SURROUNDING PLANTS

FAUNA / WILDLIFE

ADDITIONAL NOTES

DATE

LOCATION

GPS

WEATHER CONDITIONS

SPECIES / TYPE

SPECIMEN #

TOTAL LENGTH

TYPE OF FOREST

- [ ] DECIDUOUS
- [ ] CONIFEROUS
- [ ] TROPICAL
- [ ] OTHER

CAP CHARACTERISTICS

CAP COLOR

CAP SHAPE

CAP TEXTURE

CAP DIAMETER

CAP LENGTH

HYMENIUM

SPECIAL PROPERTIES

STALK CHARACTERISTICS

STALK COLOR

STALK SHAPE

STALK TEXTURE

STALK DIAMETER

STALK LENGTH

STALK SURFACE

SPECIAL PROPERTIES

SURROUNDING PLANTS

FAUNA / WILDLIFE

ADDITIONAL NOTES

Made in the USA
Coppell, TX
11 January 2023

10923717R00069